I0120955

Table of Contents

The Skillful Questioner

Problems cannot be solved by the same level of thinking that created them.
~ Albert Einstein

During the Renaissance there was a massive resurgence of learning and a gradual yet widespread shift in education, leading to economic growth and development, political and social reform, and an increase in trade and commerce.

The Industrial Revolution was a major turning point in human history. There were immense technological advancements, economic progress, income & population growth, and an increase in the standard of living never seen before.

Why?

They were asking themselves powerful questions that shifted the way they approached problems, and spurred curiosity and creativity.

Today, we are on the verge of another major shift. To make the leap we need to make we must ask ourselves and our clients questions that achieve & surpass that same level of curiosity and creativity.

The quality of questions we ask directly influence the knowledge we acquire and the actions we take.

By asking quality, empowering questions we can find the answers leading to the change we seek.

Being a skillful questioner is more than just the words used in the questions. It's as much about how you ask the questions as it is about the words you use. Having no attachment to the outcome of the question and addressing the questioner with curiosity, objectivity and in a non-confrontational manner creates an atmosphere of safety for the questionee to answer honestly and thoroughly.

With over 30 years of coaching, training, facilitation, and experiential learning experience between the two of them, both Denny & Kathy Jo recognize even the most skilled professionals can sometimes get stuck finding the right questions.

Asking powerful questions allow the questionee to see things differently, open up creativity, gain new perspectives, see solutions, discover their own answers, deepens relationships and trust, and improves problem-solving and decision-making abilities.

You can ask the most empowering questions and unlock amazing possibilities, but unless you truly listen and the questionee feels that intent, forward movement is stunted. Listening is an important part of communication as is asking powerful questions. However, not all listening is effective listening.

It is said that hearing is a physical ability. We all hear. We don't always listen. Listening is a skill, one that must be practiced and intentional to be effective.

As a vital part of the questioning process, listening enables:
- The acquisition of new information
- Greater insight to the values, strengths, behavior and needs of the questionee
- The questionee to discover his / her own perspectives of the situation
- Trust & Rapport
- Understanding of underlying meaning
- Motivation
- Depth & Intimacy
- Mutual understanding
- The questionee to feel heard and understood

Levels of Listening

There are 4 Levels of Listening. We have all experienced listening to others and being listened to at each level. The higher the level the more energy is required to maintain that level. Not every conversation you have will take place at the Intuitive Listening level.

1. **Competitive Listening**: The main focus in Competitive Listening is on the listener's own thoughts. Here the listener is more interested in their own views and is waiting for an opportunity to jump in and react.

2. **Attentive Listening**: The main focus in Attentive Listening is on the words being said. There is genuine interest in hearing and understanding what is being said but assumes an understanding, not checking with the questionee for confirmation.

3. **Reflective Listening**: The main focus in Reflective Listening is on a deeper and clarified understanding of what is being said. There is genuine interest in listening, not just hearing, as well as understanding what is being said and confirms that understanding, often through mirroring back the exact information shared.

4. **Intuitive Listening**: The main focus in Intuitive Listening is an understanding of the meaning behind what is said. There is genuine desire to understand not only the meaning of what is being said but also the tone, pitch, speed, of what's being said, the body language that accompanies the words, what is being said behind the words, and what is NOT being said.

We all know how important communication is. However, the vast majority of communication isn't spoken. According to studies done in the '70s by Albert Mehrabian, only 7% of communication takes place through exchange of words. The remaining 93% of information is communicated through body language, eye contact, and pitch, speed, tone and volume of the voice.

Understanding that most information is not communicated through words, to be a powerful listener there are several things you have to keep in mind while listening to the questionee.

Keys to Powerful Listening

1. Intentions are set to gain a greater understanding of the questionee, their behavior, thinking, values, beliefs, perspectives and needs.
2. Stay Curious.
3. Detached Involvement: the ability to tap into deep levels of empathy and place yourself in the questionees position, understanding their thoughts and feelings without taking on their emotions.
4. Focus on what is being communicated in all areas – body language, tone, pace, pitch, energy – while not focusing on your response.
5. Offer feedback and request clarification if necessary.
6. Remember silence is golden. Don't be afraid of silence. Allow the questionee to sit with the question and ponder.
7. Use Intuitive Listening as much as possible.

When entering a conversation where you are required to deeply listen and understand questionees, try your best to enter the situation with as much energy as possible.

Powerful Questions + Intuitive Listening + Acknowledgement + Time to Respond = Unlocked Potential & Possibilities

Making Questions Powerful

Asking the right questions in the right way is key to achieving the right results. Powerful questions immediately access our creative, holistic brain, from which solutions are born. These thought provoking questions are designed to forward your client's actions through clarifying, inspiring, probing, challenging, affirming, exploring, opening new possibilities, connecting, assessing, and evaluating, leading to the right solutions for your client.

When crafting questions, there are 3 things you must consider.
1. The Scope of the Question
2. The Construction of the Question
3. Assumptions & Bias in the Question

Scope

The Scope is defined as the range or subject matter that something either deals with or to which it is relevant. The scope covers the domain of inquiry. Matching the scope of the question to meet the needs of inquiry increases the capacity to effect change and sets the questionee up for success. Therefore, keep within realistic boundaries of the situation and questionee's knowledge and power.

For example: "How can you best change your perspective?" as opposed to "How can you change the perspective within the organization?"

When determining the scope of your question you must first determine the scope of the answer you are seeking. If you are looking for greater clarification you must ask questions designed to gain that clarity. If you are looking for greater insight, you must ask questions designed to go deeper. If you are looking to at obstacles you must ask questions designed to uncover blocks. The scope of the answer determines the category of the question to achieve an appropriate response. You can find the question categories under the General Questions section of this book.

Construction

The construction of a question consists of the language, intention and tone you take when asking the question. A question's construction is a critical element in either opening up one's mind to possibilities or closing the mind to solutions. The construction of a question can determine the depth and direction of the answers. Are you looking for a direct yes or no answer? Ask a closed-ended question. Are you looking for deeper clarification? Do you want to open choices or create a new picture? Ask open-ended questions.

The construction of a question stimulates reflective thinking and deepens the conversation. Starting your question with either "who" or "how" determines the level and direction of inquiry. For example: "Who can help you to make this happen?" "How can this happen?"

When constructing the question, ask yourself what "work" you want this question to do.

Assumptions and Bias

Part of being human is that our experiences and perspectives influence the way we think. We all carry with us assumptions and biases. We cannot eliminate them. Awareness of assumptions and biases allow us to be on the look-out for them as we construct and ask our questions, and listen to the answer.

One of the most commonly used questions containing an assumption and bias is "What is wrong?" This question assumes a negative.

Reframing is a potent way to reword questions freeing them of assumptions and bias such as from "What's wrong?" to "What happened?" Reframing encourages deeper reflection and shifts assumptions into possibilities for creating forward action.

A Word About "Why"

Some of the most powerful questions begin with "Why." Some of the most dangerous questions begin with "Why."

Why-questions can lead to greater insight and more thorough answers. They ask the questionee to go deeper inside and evaluate. Answers to why-questions speak about the inner feelings, beliefs, and motives of the questionee. Because of the highly personal nature of why-questions if safely and trust have yet to be established in the relationship a why-question can easily trigger reactive behaviors and blame detracting from solutions.

The difference between getting greater insight and triggering reaction is the level of safety the questionee feels in the relationship and the way in which the question is asked.

If safety and trust have been established on both sides of the relationship and a why-question is the most appropriate question to ask, stay curious when asking your question. This will keep the non-verbal elements of asking a question as well as your intention on

Choose why-questions carefully and sparingly.

Characteristics of a Powerful Question

1. Solutions-focused
2. Clear & Simple
3. Involves Values & Ideals
4. Generates Curiosity
5. Stimulates Reflection
6. Thought-Provoking
7. Engages Attention
8. Focused
9. Touches Deeper Meaning
10. Leads to More Questions

How to Use This Book

As you encounter a specific challenge around leadership in your life, or your client's or employee's life, you may become stuck and not know where to go next. This book is designed to assist in getting unstuck by sparking new, unique, and in-depth questions. Use these questions as is or allow them to inspire new ideas for you.

Open / Closed-Ended Questions Chart: Open-Ended questions are designed to require the answerer to go deeper and give more detail. These types of questions should be used as often as possible to gain greater detail, inquiry, and increase understanding. Closed-Ended questions are excellent for commitment. These are used ONLY when looking for a "yes" or "no" response.

General Leadership Questions: The general Leadership-based questions are a great starting point for coaching around Leadership issues. These questions are designed around a basic coaching approach of: clarifying, creating a vision, defining choice, identifying blocks and barriers, evaluating, prioritizing, probing, and scaling. Use these questions as touch-stones throughout the process. Categorized based on your client's specific needs and situation, these questions increase the scope of the coaching relationship.

Leadership Wheel: The Leadership Wheel is a self-awareness assessment you can use for yourself or your client to rate the level of satisfaction in each area of Leadership. Use the Wheel to broaden the scope of coaching through encompassing each area to create the ideal Leadership style.

Wheel Specific Questions: As your partnership deepens and gaps in leadership skills present themselves, target different areas of leadership more thoroughly through these questions. Use Wheel Specific questions to prolong the coaching partnership and develop a more conscious Leader.

Leadership Values / Qualities Assessment: Rate Leadership Values / Qualities by how important they are to you or your client, and how much you walk your talk can help identify where gaps may be in Leadership Skills. This is an excellent resource in identifying areas and opportunities for growth.

Blank Wheel: Using the Blank Wheel, fill in your or your client's top 8 Leadership Values / Qualities and rank these to address the gaps of creating the ideal Leader. You can also develop new coaching assignments and opportunities around each area.

Leadership Quotes: This collection of Leadership Quotes is a great resource for either your own marketing efforts or to deepen the level of thinking for your clients. Use these quotes to send inspirational emails, add to your website, use as topics for your newsletters or to Tweet.

SMART Goals Checklist: Goals help ensure success. Goals that are unattainable or unreasonable are a direct line to failure. Failure stifles excitement, passion, and commitment. To ensure the success of your clients, check each goal against the SMART Goals checklist to determine how viable the goal truly is and keep your client's on track.

Additional Uses for This Book

Coaching / Consulting Role

→ Use the Leadership Wheel Assessment in a Complementary Session

→ Assess a client's level of satisfaction in the 8 key areas of the Leadership Wheel in an introductory session to establish the partnership foundation

→ Use SMART Goals checklist as an evaluation & progression tool

→ Create accountability around the SMART Goals checklist

→ Identify strengths & gaps in each area of the Leadership Wheel

→ Identify initial coaching goals

→ Use the questions as preparation for coaching sessions

→ Create customized assignments using the questions

→ Create visualizations & meditations based around the Leadership Wheel segments or Questions

→ Use quotes in sessions to stimulate fresh perspectives

→ Add quotes to client emails for inspiration

→ Create a customized assignment by journaling on quotes

→ Create a mastermind or group discussion around a specific quote

→ Help clients set goals using the SMART Goals checklist

Product & Services Development

→ Use this book and the Leadership Wheel as your Signature Program

→ Use Leadership Wheel Assessment in a workshop as an assessment or discussion tool

→ Add Leadership Wheel Assessment to your current Signature Program or product

→ Use questions as an idea generator

→ Create an E-course / E-book / E-workbook series around segments of the Wheel

→ Develop workshops & seminars around segments of the Leadership Wheel

→ Form Mastermind Groups around key Leadership Wheel segments

→ Use Leadership Values / Qualities list as an idea generator

→ Write an E-course / E-book / E-workbook on a grouping of Leadership Values

→ Create Workshops & Seminars on a grouping of Leadership Values

→ Add a quote to a product or presentation for inspiration or point emphasis

→ Use quote in workshop as a discussion topic

→ Use SMART Goals checklist in a workshop as tool to move participants forward

Marketing / Business Development

→ Use Leadership Wheel Assessment as a prospect pre-qualifier

→ Create a prequalifying survey for prospects with questions

→ Use Leadership Questions or Quotes in ezine / newsletter

→ Post a Leadership Question / Quote to your target audience on a LinkedIn Discussion

→ Use a series of Leadership Questions to outline a promotional teleclass

→ Create a free download of Leadership Questions around a particular topic

→ Use questions in Blog & Twitter Posts

→ Write an article based on the Leadership Questions

→ Write an article based on an individual Leadership Value

→ Use the Leadership Values Assessment as a pre-coaching prep form

→ Create an ezine / newsletter around an individual Leadership Value

→ Post a quote on your blog / Facebook / LinkedIn asking for comments

→ Use a quote to inspire a podcast or video

→ Use quote to motivate an article idea

→ Post Quote on Blog / Twitter

Open-Ended vs. Closed-Ended Questions

Open-Ended questions invite others to discuss in detail what is important to them. They are used to gather information, establish rapport, and increase understanding. These questions do not lead and are not geared towards expected outcomes. When used, the asker must be willing to listen and respond appropriately.

Closed-Ended questions are used to elicit a definitive answer. Use only when you want a definite yes or no. They are particularly useful when gaining a commitment.

Ask Open-Ended questions whenever possible.

Open-Ended Questions Start with:	Closed-Ended Questions Start with:
Who	Is
What	Does
How	Are
Why	Do
When	Will
Where	Can

General Leadership Questions

Clarifying

Clarifying questions are designed to lay the groundwork and foundation for attaining goals. They set the stage, remove ambiguity, elicit details, and supply known facts.

Ask Clarifying Questions when you need a clear picture of where the questionee is currently at, what resources are available, what perspectives they have, as well as want a picture of where the questionee is coming from, what they want, and the reality of the situation.

Ask these questions as a starting point, to establish a framework.

Example of Clarifying Questions

Questionee: I want to feel more freedom in my life.

Questioner: What do you mean by more freedom?

Questionee: I mean to have the ability to do what I want when I want to.

Questioner: Give me an example.

Clarifying Questions

→ Who would you model your leadership style after?

→ Who do you admire as a leader?

→ Who on your team supplements your leadership skills?

→ Who has made an impact on your life?

→ What does leadership mean to you?

→ What is leadership?

→ What is leadership not?

→ With what type of leader do you work best?

→ What's taking shape here?

→ What do you see as your role?

→ What are recurring challenges or issues that keep popping up?

→ What allowed that positive experience to happen?

→ What path are you currently on?

→ What does a leader do?

→ What kind of leadership works best?

→ What is a hard leader?

→ What is a soft leader?

→ What is your role as a leader?

→ As a leader, to what are you most committed?

→ What does servant-leadership mean to you?

→ What are you most proud of accomplishing as a leader?

→ What about your leadership style is working well for you now?

→ Where are you not seeing the full picture?

→ Where is your leadership style most appreciated?

→ When was the first time you took on the role of a leader?

→ How did you do that?

→ How do you express your leadership?

→ How do you lead?

→ How do you like to be lead?

→ How do you define leadership?

→ How clear are you on what makes a good leader?

→ How do you share your leadership gifts?

→ How do you know when leadership falls short?

→ How do you know when it excels?

→ How are you a servant-leader?

→ How do you model leadership for others?

→ How do you normally deal with adversity?

→ How do you normally deal with change?

Visioning

Visioning questions are designed to establish a desired end result. These questions create a picture of the future so a plan on how to get there can be created.

Visioning Questions allow the questionee to "see" the result they are working to achieve. This opens possibilities, engages creativity, and keeps motivation high and direction clear.

Ask Visioning Questions when creating a new reality, establishing an end-result, identifying the ideal, or giving direction to move forward.

Example of Visioning Questions

Questioner: What would you ideally like to see happen?

Questionee: I would like to move to the country away from the noise and congestion of the city. I would like to grow my own food, and live more simply. I would like to see the stars at night and hear the crickets sing.

Questioner: In this ideal vision, what do you see yourself doing?

Questionee: I see myself writing that book I keep talking about and having time to putter around in my flower garden.

Questioner: How would you feel if you had that?

Questionee: I see myself really happy, living a good life with the people I love, enjoying the things that give my life meaning.

Questioner: That is a beautiful picture for you.

Questionee: Yes it is!

Visioning Questions

→ Who shouldn't be a leader?

→ Who makes the best leaders?

→ If you were in your advanced years and had an opportunity to tell a fresh-out-of-college young adult the most important thing you learned about being a leader in your life, what you tell them?

→ What does leadership look like on the playground?

→ In the classroom?

→ In the boardroom?

→ If someone led purely from the head, what would that look like?

→ If someone led purely from the heart, what would that look like?

→ What would a combination of the two look like?

→ What does a leader look like?

→ What makes an ideal leader?

→ What should a leader be passionate about?

→ What type of organization cultivates empowered leaders?

→ What type of leader cultivates empowered organizations?

→ Where have you seen leadership at its best?

→ When was the last time you say someone lead in a positive way?

→ Without them saying a word, how can to tell someone is a leader?

→ How do you inspire & motivate others through leadership?

→ How would you want to lead?

→ How do you need to change your leadership style?

→ How can you address this situation where it works for everyone?

→ How can you be the most effective leader?

→ How can you improve your leadership style?

Choice

Choice Questions are meant to show options, empower, and accept responsibility. These questions lend to out-of-the-box thinking and demonstrate options and opportunities.

Ask Choice Questions when questionee feels trapped, hopeless, or feels as though there is no other answer, and needs a new perspective & empowerment to move forward.

Example of Choice Questions

Questionee: I don't know what to do. I really would like to attend that seminar next Saturday and Sunday but my husband wants to take the kids to the cabin that same weekend. We always do everything together.

Questioner: If you knew no-one would be upset, what options do you have to resolve this?

Questionee: You mean, if I went to the seminar and my husband took the boys to the cabin without me?

Questioner: What would happen if that could be the reality?

Questionee: Well that certainly would be different. Maybe that would work. I will talk with my husband tonight.

Choice Questions

→   Whose leadership style do you not want to emulate?

→   Who is ultimately responsible?

→   What would you do differently next time?

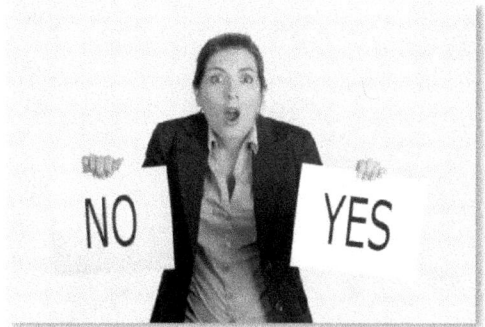

→   What other choices are available?

→   What resources do you have available?

→   What is your objective for doing this?

→   What can you do as an effective leader?

→   What would it take to create change in this situation?

→   What challenges might come your way and how might you deal with them?

→   What is the right action for you to take in this situation?

→   What are you choosing not to see?

→   If success was guaranteed, what bold steps might you choose right now?

→   Where do you want this to go?

→   Where do you not need to wear the hat of a leader?

→   When can you relax as a leader?

→   When does this decision need to be made?

→   Why do you need to do that now?

→   Why are you a servant-leader?

→   Why do you prefer being a conscious leader?

→   Why do you lead?

Blocks & Barriers

These questions are designed to uncover and examine what is stopping the questionee from moving forward, seeing progress, and gaining what they truly want.

Ask Blocks and Barrier Questions when you sense hesitation, resistance, goal hopping, or a belief they are unable to move forward.

Example of Blocks & Barriers Questions

Questionee: I really would like to date again but can't seem to put myself out there.

Questioner: What do you think is getting in the way?

Questionee: I'm not sure.....maybe my fear.

Questioner: Fear of what?

Questionee: Fear of not being attractive enough....of no one being interested in me.

Questioner: So you would rather stay home alone where it is safe than risk getting rejected again.

Questionee: As pitiful as that sounds, yes, I think that is it.

Questioner: How well will that work for you?

Questionee: Not very well at all since I want to meet someone! I guess we have some more work to do!

Questioner: I guess we do!

Blocks & Barriers Questions

→ Who is your biggest challenge?

→ Who gets in the way of your productivity as a leader?

→ What about these beliefs stops you?

→ What internal or external blocks do you have that hold you back from being an ideal leader?

→ What is the biggest leadership challenge today?

→ What makes that challenge particularly difficult?

→ What is the hardest thing about leading well?

→ What thoughts come up for you when you think of being a leader?

→ What thoughts come up for you when you think of being a follower?

→ Where do you feel inadequate?

→ Where do you stop yourself?

→ Where do you have difficulties making the tough decisions?

→ Where else does this come up for you?

→ When are you overwhelmed with the responsibility of being a leader?

→ Why do you feel you're not a good leader?

→ Why does the idea of leading the way bother you?

→ Why is this such a struggle?

→ How do your beliefs of what a strong leader is get in the way of being an effective leader?

→ How are you limiting yourself?

→ How do your assumptions of this situation affect the way you are leading?

→ How did you interpret that?

Evaluating

Evaluating Questions determine criteria. They evaluate or estimate the nature, quality, extent or significance of situations. They assess factors such as needs, issues, processes, performance, and outcomes. They can also determine the pros & cons of a situation.

Ask Evaluating Questions when the questionee needs to establish a clearer sense of their wants and needs related to a particular situation.

Example of Evaluating Questions

Questionee: I want to achieve more success at work.

Questioner: What would that look like?

Questionee: I would work more efficiently and get things done on time.

Questioner: What would be different if you were more efficient?

Questionee: I would lead meetings with more confidence and get more buy-in from the team.

Questioner: How would it feel if you achieved all of that?

Questionee: Great!

Evaluating Questions

→ Who do you believe is an ideal leader?

→ Who do you believe is a less than ideal leader?

→ Who is a leader?

→ Who in history would you say was the perfect leader?

→ Who can be a leader?

→ What place should consciousness have in leadership?

→ What would a highly conscious leader do?

→ What would a highly conscious leader avoid?

→ What does a leader never, ever do?

→ What inspires leaders to do their best?

→ What motivates leaders to make the tough decisions?

→ What skills are needed to be an effective leader?

→ What are qualities and characteristics of an effective leader?

→ If you had to describe leadership in just three words, what would you say?

→ Where should a leader be passionate?

→ When does it succeed?

→ When should a leader step down?

→ When should a leader step up?

→ When does leadership fail?

→ Why should organizations have strong leadership?

→ How important is it to be an effective leader?

→ How effective of a leader are you?

→ How strong are your leadership skills?

→ How well do you fit into your idea of an ideal leader?

→ How do you measure your success as a leader?

→ How do power and leadership relate?

→ How is leadership learned?

Goal Setting

Goal Setting Questions are designed to move into and forward the action. They include aspects of accountability, step-by-step action, and an understanding of what needs to be done in order to accomplish the desired goal(s).

Goal Setting Questions are intended to set the questionee up for success. In order to accomplish this there are certain factors to be considered when designing a goal plan.

SMART Goals help construct a format for creating successful goals.

Ask Goal Setting Questions when the questionee is ready to move into action.

Example of Goal Setting Questions

Questionee: I decided I want to return to college and finish my degree.

Questioner: That's great! When would you like to begin?

Questionee: Next semester but I have some things I need to do first.

Questioner: What do you see as the 1st step to take to get started?

Questionee: Well, I need to talk with an admissions counselor and figure out what credits will transfer and how many credits I need to complete my degree. Then I have to decide which classes to start with.

Questioner: That sounds like a plan. When will you make the appointment?

Questionee: This week. I am excited!
    (Move onto creating SMART Goals *pg. 65)

Goal Setting Questions

→ Who can help you get started?

→ From whom do you need that information?

→ What would you do if you knew you could not fail?

→ What is the first step you need to take?

→ What other skills or resources do you need to accomplish that?

→ What do you need to make this happen?

→ What systems need to be in place?

→ What are the milestones to reaching this goal?

→ What would be a stretch for you?

→ What is one thing you can do this week that will clearly demonstrate your commitment to your goal?

→ Where will this take you?

→ Where do conscious leaders finish first?

→ When do you want to achieve this?

→ When will you start?

→ When can you ask for help?

→ When in the past were you successful?

→ Why is it important to reach this?

→ Why not start now?

→ Why start now?

→ Why would that make a difference?

→ How can you make that happen?

→ How can being conscious about your leadership make that happen faster?

→ How do you want to lead?

→ How can you fill the gaps between your ideal leader image and where you are currently at?

→ How will these steps move you closer to your goal?

Prioritizing

Prioritizing Questions identifies and weighs importance, values and benefits. They can also be used to rank & order.

Prioritizing Questions are great to use in conjunction with Goal Setting Questions and can also help reduce overwhelm.

Ask Prioritizing Questions when the questionee needs to put their priorities in order or examine what is important to them.

Example of Prioritizing Questions

Questionee: I have so many things I need to get done. I feel overwhelmed!

Questioner: That is understandable considering all you have on your plate. Let's make a list of everything you have to do.

Questionee: OK.

(Together they create a list of 'to-do's')

Questionee: That's a lot! No wonder I feel overwhelmed.

Questioner: I hear you! Let's chunk it down. Of these 12 items, which are the most urgent and necessary to get done this week?

Questionee: I would have to say numbers 3, 6 and 7. The others can wait. I feel much better.

Prioritizing Questions

→ Who would you prefer on your team?

→ To whom can you release that?

→ Who will be first?

→ What aspect of leadership is more important, the head or the heart?

→ What comes first?

→ What are the top 3-5 must-haves for any leader?

→ What is the most effective leadership style?

→ Where do you start?

→ When is being a soft leader necessary?

→ When is being a hard leader necessary?

→ When is being a caring leader necessary?

→ When is it important to just listen?

→ When is it important to step up?

→ When is it important to sit back?

→ When is leadership important?

→ Why is that important to you?

→ Why is leadership important?

→ In the grand scheme of things, how important is leadership really?

→ How do you make tough decisions as a leader?

Probing

Probing Questions make the questionee go deeper, drawing out more details, concerns, challenges, knowledge, and issues about a particular situation. A good Probing Question requires thought. These questions are used to get out the root of the situation, and reveal thoughts, feelings, and details under the surface.

Ask Probing Questions when going deeper into an issue or concern will bring greater insight and help uncover new awareness; thoughts and feelings lying below the surface.

Example of Probing Questions

Questionee: I really don't want to do my presentation tomorrow.

Questioner: Why not?

Questionee: I don't know. Even though I put a lot of time into preparing it, I guess I don't think it's very good. I'd rather hold off until I can make it better.

Questioner: From what you described last time, it appears you have a solid presentation.

Questionee: Yeah, I guess so. I just think it could be better.

Questioner: Putting the presentation itself aside, what are you really worried about?

Questionee: (Pause) That I will freeze...nothing will come out of my mouth and look like a bumbling fool!

Questioner: That is quite a worry.

Questionee: I didn't realize how anxious I am about speaking to the group.

Questioner: How would it be for us to work on that together?

Questionee: Yes, please! It would be great.

Probing Questions

→ Who do you admire most as a leader? Why?

→ What beliefs do you have around leadership?

→ What effects do these beliefs have on your role as a leader or your life?

→ What beliefs do you have about yourself as a leader?

→ What are your core values as a leader?

→ What qualities do admired leaders possess?

→ What would you change about your leadership abilities?

→ What makes you believe you are a good leader?

→ What talents or skills make you a good leader?

→ What is your leadership style?

→ What are your gifts as a leader?

→ Where do you need to improve as a leader?

→ Where do you limit yourself as a leader?

→ How comfortable are you when being a leader?

→ How much do your thoughts affect your ability to lead?

→ How has being a leader changed you?

New Perspectives

New Perspective Questions are designed to shift the direction of thinking. By shifting thinking the questionee can shift the way they approach the world and situations. These questions often create "aha" moments as they elicit options and possibilities previously not considered.

Ask New Perspective Questions when the questionee persists in levels of thinking that include anger, blame, victim, trapped or when they are unable / unwilling to see alternatives.

Example of New Perspective Questions

Questionee: I think my sister is upset with me.

Questioner: What makes you think that?

Questionee: Because she hasn't returned my calls this week.

Questioner: How certain are you she is upset with you?

Questionee: Well, why else wouldn't she call me back?

Questioner: Great question! What might be some other reasons she hasn't called you back yet?

Questionee: Well, maybe she's really busy with work. I know she had a big project she was working on and her boss can set some tough deadlines. I bet that's it.

New Perspectives Questions

→ What would it take to be a good leader?

→ If an organization had no leadership, what would happen?

→ What difference does an effective leader make?

→ What core masculine qualities should a leader possess?

→ What core feminine qualities should a leader possess?

→ If you were to use a geometric shape to describe leadership within an organization, what shape would you chose and why?

→ If effective leadership was an energetic force, what would that be?

→ What type of leadership style is most advantageous to creative problem-solving?

→ Where do you find leadership?

→ Where can you use your leadership skills?

→ Where can you use your leadership skills to make the biggest difference?

→ When you become the type of leader you want to be, what will be different?

→ When is leadership a straight line?

→ When is it a curve?

→ Why must you be a strong leader?

→ Why are you a leader?

→ How can you shift your beliefs about leadership / your role as a leader / leadership styles to better serve you?

Scaling

Scaling Questions help gauge and determine the level of concern, commitment, and importance. They are a tool that identifies where the questionee would position themselves, the situation or determining a level. Scaling Questions can be used to help measure progress, attitude and behavioral change, and situational shifts.

Ask Scaling Questions when the questionee wants to gauge the level of concern, commitment, or importance of a situation or concern.

Example of Scaling Questions

Questioner: On a scale of 1-10, 1 being not at all and 10 being extremely, how important is that for you?

Questionee: I would say about an 8.5.

Questioner: That's pretty important!

Questionee: Yes, it really it.

Scaling Questions

→ On a Scale of 1 to 10 (10=is the ideal leader and 1=lacks leadership skills) where would you rank yourself as an influential leader? Why did you rank yourself that way?

→ On a Scale of 1 to 10 (10=completely and 1=not at all) how well do your beliefs of yourself as a leader work for you? Why did you rank yourself that way?

→ On a Scale of 1 to 10 (10=completely and 1=not at all) how comfortable are you in being a leader? Why did you rank yourself that way?

→ On a Scale of 1 to 10 (10=completely and 1=not at all) where do you rank yourself as a conscious leader? Why did you rank yourself that way?

→ On a Scale of 1 to 10 (10=completely and 1=not at all) how much responsibility do you carry as a leader? Why did you rank yourself that way?

→ On a Scale of 1 to 10 (10=completely and 1=not at all) how comfortable are you in making the tough decisions? Why did you rank yourself that way?

→ On a Scale of 1 to 10 (10=completely and 1=not at all) how comfortable are you delegating? Why did you rank yourself that way?

→ On a Scale of 1 to 10 (10=completely and 1=not at all) how comfortable are you being responsible for making decisions? Why did you rank yourself that way?

→ On a Scale of 1 to 10 (10=Master and 1=Beginner) where would you rank yourself in your listening skills? Why did you rank yourself that way?

→ On a Scale of 1 to 10 (10=completely and 1=not at all) how comfortable are you managing others? Why did you rank yourself that way?

Leadership Wheel Assessment

Directions: for each section of the Leadership Wheel, circle the number that represents your current level of satisfaction in that area. The higher the number, the greater your level of satisfaction.

LEADERSHIP

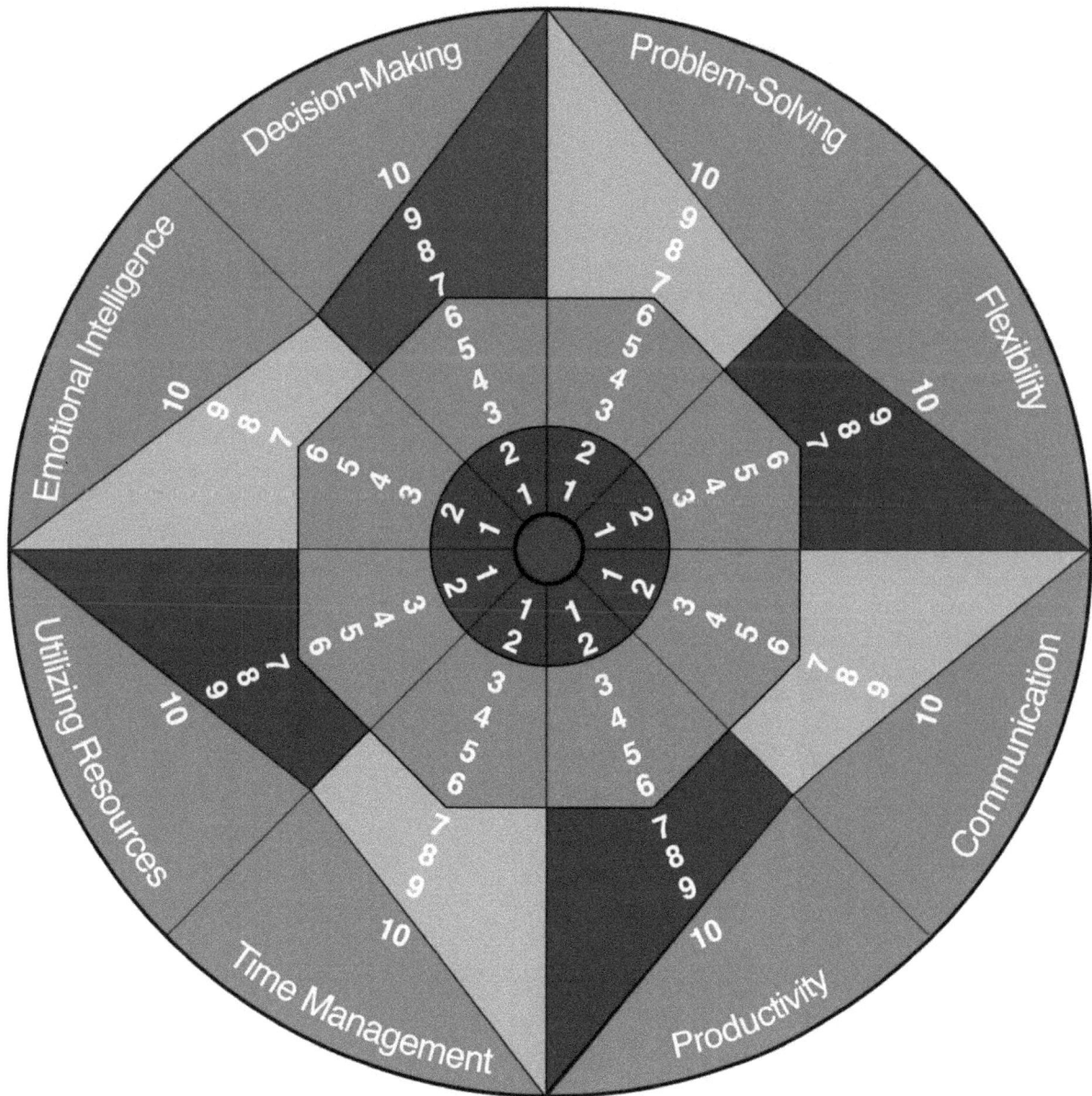

Flexibility

Who

→ Who would you be without flexibility?

→ Who epitomizes flexibility to you?

→ With whom do you have the most difficult time being flexible? Why?

→ With whom do you have the easiest time being flexible? Why?

→ Who in your organization needs flexibility the most?

What

→ What does flexibility mean to you as a leader?

→ What are the benefits of being a flexible leader?

→ What is the downside?

→ What three qualities identify a flexible leader?

→ What could you do to become more flexible in your role?

Where

→ Where do you need to be more flexible?

→ Where do you need to be less flexible?

→ Where do you need to be unbendable?

→ Where is flexibility weakest in your organization?

→ Where is flexibility the strongest?

When

→ When is flexibility most essential?

→ When is flexibility a liability?

→ When would you use flexibility to gain the best results?

→ When, as a leader, are you most flexible?

→ When are you the least?

Why

→ Why is it important to be flexible as a leader?

→ Why is flexibility helpful in an organization?

→ Why does effective leadership require flexibility?

→ Why is flexibility useful?

→ Why would a leader choose not to be flexible?

How

→ How flexible are you?

→ How do you adjust to change?

→ How will being flexible help you in your role as a leader?

→ How can flexibility be cultivated?

→ How would a team benefit from flexible leadership?

Your Questions on Flexibility

→ _____

→ _____

→ _____

→ _____

Communication

Who

→ Who is your ideal communicator? Why?

→ With whom are you having a communication challenge?

→ With whom do you need to communicate more?

→ With whom do you need to communicate less?

→ Who benefits the most from effective communication?

What

→ What is effective communication?

→ What needs to happen for there to be effective communication?

→ What happens as a result of effective communication?

→ What needs communicated the most?

→ What is your communication style?

Where

→ Where does communication tend to break down for you?

→ Where are you comfortable communicating your needs?

→ Where is your communication comfort zone?

→ Where do you need to communicate more? Of what?

→ Where do you need to communicate less? Of what?

When

→ When is the right time to listen?

→ When in the right time to speak?

→ When is clear communication the hardest to achieve?

→ When does communication work best?

→ When is transparent communication essential?

Why

→ Why is effective communication important in leadership?

→ Why does a leader need to be an effective communicator?

→ Why do you need to communicate more effectively?

→ Why is clear communication difficult to achieve?

→ Why should you invest the time required to communicate effectively?

How

→ How does your communication style affect your leadership skills?

→ How is your communication style received by others?

→ How can you improve your communication skills?

→ How does your leadership style affect your communication style?

→ How would others benefit from effective communication?

Your Questions on Communication

→ _____

→ _____

→ _____

→ _____

Productivity

Who

→ Whose help is needed to accomplish your goals?

→ Who defines success for this project?

→ Who can help you take action?

→ Who inspires you to do more? Why?

→ Who de-motivates you? Why?

What

→ What strategies can you implement to increase your productivity?

→ What needs to happen for you to be more productive?

→ What does productivity mean to you?

→ What comes to mind when you think of being productive?

→ What do you need to change to achieve your productivity goals?

Where

→ Where are you most productive?

→ Where are you least productive?

→ Where do you feel energized?

→ Where are your attentions diverted?

→ Where are your barriers to productivity?

When

→ When are you excited about getting stuff done?

→ When are you the most productive?

→ When do you achieve ideal results?

→ When do you find yourself disengaging?

→ When do you need to be done?

Why

→ Why are you excited about being productive?

→ Why is getting things done important to you?

→ Why can leaders get bogged down?

→ Why is being productive necessary as a leader?

→ Why are attention and intention necessary parts of productivity?

How

→ How do you measure productivity?

→ How do you measure efficiency?

→ How can you utilize the resources you currently have available to achieve your goals?

→ How can you implement production strategies?

→ How do you inhibit your own productivity?

Your Questions on Productivity

→ _____

→ _____

→ _____

Decision-Making

Who

→ Who is responsible for the ultimate decision for this project?

→ Who do you need input from to make a conscious decision?

→ Who is avoiding a decision right now?

→ Who is fighting a decision right now?

→ Who brings perspective to the decision-making table?

What

→ What skills do you need to be effective at decision-making?

→ What creates barriers to decision-making?

→ What influences your decisions?

→ What opportunities for growth do you see in your decision-making abilities?

→ What would effortless decision-making look like to you?

Where

→ Where do you resist making decision?

→ Where does a decision need to be made?

→ Where do you experience doubt in your decisions?

→ Where do you need more information to make this decision?

→ Where does your attention need to be to make your decision?

When

→ When are you afraid to make a decision? Why?

→ When are you confident in your decision-making abilities?

→ When are your decisions best supported? Why?

→ When are they the least supported? Why?

→ When have you felt the absolute best about a decision you made?

Why

→ Why is decision-making important as a leader?

→ Why is decision-making sometimes like a roller coaster ride?

→ Why do you sometimes shy away from making decisions?

→ Why do you feel pressured to make quick decisions?

→ Why is making decisions so difficult at times?

How

→ How does your leadership style affect your decision-making abilities?

→ How willing are you to make tough decisions?

→ How can you see an opportunity within this difficulty?

→ How is decision-making related to problem management?

→ How can the decision-making process be easier?

Your Questions on Decision-making

→ _____

→ _____

→ _____

→ _____

Problem Solving

Who

→ Who can assist you in solving your challenges?

→ With whom do you avoid conflict?

→ With whom do you find yourself in a tangle?

→ Who is pointing the finger at you? Why?

→ Who do you have to become to see all problems as opportunities?

What

→ What is your greatest challenge?

→ What thoughts come up for you when thinking of this challenge?

→ What beliefs influence your problem solving abilities?

→ What is different about you when seeing solutions instead of challenges?

→ What do you need to let go of, move through, or face to address this challenge?

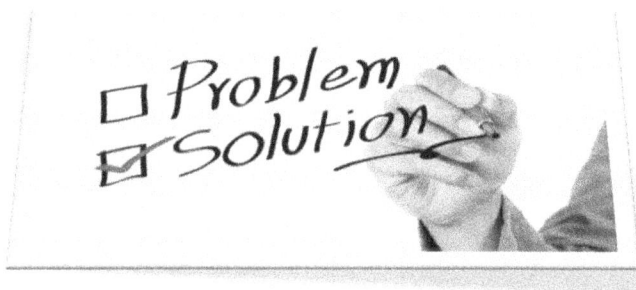

Where

→ Where are your greatest challenges?

→ Where can you shift perspectives about these challenges?

→ Where do you need to improve your problem solving skills?

→ Where might you be stressed, frustrated, or worried?

→ Where might it serve you to let go of stress, frustration, or worry?

When

→ When do you ignore, deny, or hide from challenges?

→ When do you fight when confronted with a challenge?

→ When do you see problems?

→ When do you see opportunities?

→ When do you see solutions?

Why

→ Why do you care?

→ Why do you want to solve this problem?

→ Why would you feel better if this were no longer an issue?

→ Why were you drawn into that conflict?

→ Why have you decided to face this problem head on?

How

→ How do you usually react to problems?

→ How would you prefer to react to problems?

→ How do you look for solutions?

→ How can you alter your perspective of your experience?

→ How many things do you worry about that are not worth it?

Your Questions on Problem Solving

→ _____

→ _____

→ _____

→ _____

→ _____

Resources

Who

→ Who are you under-utilizing as a resource?

→ From whom can you reliably ask for help?

→ Who is someone to avoid asking for help? Why?

→ Who can become your best ally?

→ To whom would you most like to reach out? Why?

What

→ What resources do you have available to you?

→ What resources do you need to achieve your goals?

→ What skills can you acquire?

→ What strengths do others have you can utilize?

→ What skills do you have that you are under-utilizing?

Where

→ Where can you find additional resources?

→ Where do you need more help right now?

→ Where would you be without that help?

→ Where is your greatest resource?

→ Where have you cultivated support?

When

→ When do you need help most?

→ When do you need help least?

→ When would someone know you need assistance?

→ When have you drawn on your resources most often?

→ When are resources the most valuable to you?

Why

→ Why are resources necessary for a leader?

→ Why reach out for support?

→ Why are you dealing with this alone?

→ Why should others want to help you?

→ Why would you use resources in your role?

How

→ How do you utilize the resources available to you?

→ How do you show appreciation for your resources?

→ How do you rely on the strengths of others?

→ How open are you to receiving help from others?

→ How often do you rely on others?

Your Questions on Resources

→ _____

→ _____

→ _____

→ _____

→ _____

Emotional Intelligence

Who

→ Who sets you off? Why?

→ Who calms you down? Why?

→ Who makes you feel small or insignificant? Why?

→ Who shows compassion towards you? Why?

→ Who makes you feel on top of the world? Why?

What

→ What is Emotional Intelligence to you?

→ What do emotions mean to you?

→ What is important about understanding how your emotions affect those around you?

→ What are your beliefs about Emotional Intelligence?

→ What impact do emotions have in your role as leader?

Where

→ Where are emotions most useful?

→ Where are emotions the least useful?

→ Where have you avoided your true feelings? Why?

→ Where have you spoken from the heart?

→ Where would you like to be more in touch with your feelings?

When

→ When are you most aware of your own emotions?

→ When are you most aware of other's emotions?

→ When do you need to be more aware of your emotions?

→ When do you need to be more aware of other's emotions?

→ When would you like to toss emotions out all together? Why?

Why

→ Why is understanding how you feel important as a leader?

→ Why have you avoided your feelings in the past?

→ Why are feelings helpful?

→ Why are feelings a hindrance?

→ Why are emotions important?

How

→ How comfortable are you when talking about emotions?

→ How can you create greater awareness of your emotions?

→ How can you create greater awareness for yourself about other people's emotions?

→ How do emotions guide your decisions?

→ How do emotions hinder your decisions?

Your Questions on Emotional Intelligence

→ _____

→ _____

→ _____

→ _____

Time Management

Who

→ Who are your time-wasters?

→ Who are your time-enhancers?

→ Who do you admire most for their time management skills?

→ Who impinges on your time?

→ Who helps you manage your time?

What

→ What does time mean to you?

→ What resources do you use to manage time?

→ What blocks your timeliness?

→ In what way does time work against you?

→ What would a well-timed day look like for you?

Where

→ Where are you most aware of time?

→ Where does the time management break down?

→ Where do you excel in managing your time?

→ Where do you fall short?

→ Where would having better time management benefit you most?

When

→ When are you usually late?

→ When are you usually on time?

→ When does time stand still for you?

→ When does time drag on and on?

→ When, in the day, are you at your best?

Why

→ Why is time your friend?

→ Why is time your enemy?

→ Why do you need to manage your time well?

→ Why have you struggled with managing your time in the past?

→ Why should time be on your side?

How

→ How do you manage your time?

→ How do you segment your time?

→ How important is time management for you as a leader?

→ How does a lack of time affect your leadership abilities?

→ How could you begin to manage your schedule better?

Your Questions on Time Management

→ _____

→ _____

→ _____

→ _____

→ _____

Leadership Values / Qualities Assessment

Directions: Identify your top 8 Values / Qualities as a Leader. How closely do you live these Values / Qualities?

☐ Acceptance	☐ Disciplined
☐ Accountability	☐ Diversifier
☐ Achievement	☐ Driven
☐ Adaptability	☐ Emotional Intelligence
☐ Ambitious	☐ Empathy
☐ Assertiveness	☐ Endurance
☐ Assertiveness	☐ Enthusiasm
☐ Authenticity	☐ Enthusiastic
☐ Candor	☐ Ethical
☐ Character	☐ Fairness
☐ Charismatic	☐ Flexibility
☐ Comfortable with Change	☐ Focused
☐ Commitment	☐ Focused
☐ Committed	☐ Follow-Through
☐ Communication Skills	☐ Forward Thinking
☐ Community Development	☐ Goal-Oriented
☐ Competency	☐ Healthy Relationships
☐ Competent	☐ Heart Guidance
☐ Consensus Builder	☐ High Energy Level
☐ Continual Learning	☐ High Expectations
☐ Co-operative	☐ High Standards
☐ Courageous	☐ Higher Consciousness
☐ Creative	☐ Holistic Thinking
☐ Creativity	☐ Honesty
☐ Critical Thinking Skills	☐ Humility
☐ Decisiveness	☐ Humor
☐ Dedication	☐ Independent
☐ Dependability	☐ Innovative

- ☐ Inspirational & Motivational
- ☐ Integrity
- ☐ Intelligent
- ☐ Interdependent
- ☐ Interpersonal Skills
- ☐ Justice
- ☐ Level-Headed
- ☐ Listener
- ☐ Loyalty
- ☐ Mature
- ☐ Mentor-Oriented
- ☐ Non-judgment of Others
- ☐ Not afraid of Adversity
- ☐ Objectivity
- ☐ Open-Door Policy
- ☐ Openness
- ☐ Opportunistic
- ☐ Optimistic
- ☐ Ownership of Actions
- ☐ Passion
- ☐ Patience
- ☐ Persuasive
- ☐ Pro-Active
- ☐ Productivity
- ☐ Purpose-Driven
- ☐ Respectful
- ☐ Responsibility
- ☐ Responsible
- ☐ Right Thinking as opposed to Wrong

- ☐ Rule-Breaker
- ☐ Rule-Oriented
- ☐ Self-Awareness
- ☐ Self-Care
- ☐ Self-Esteem
- ☐ Self-Growth
- ☐ Self-Less
- ☐ Self-Regulation
- ☐ Service-Oriented
- ☐ Setting Boundaries
- ☐ Solutions Focused
- ☐ Straightforward
- ☐ Structured
- ☐ Supportive
- ☐ Tactful
- ☐ Team Work
- ☐ Tolerance
- ☐ Tough
- ☐ Utilizing Strengths of Others
- ☐ Values-Oriented
- ☐ Visionary
- ☐ Visionary
- ☐ Willing to Take Risks
- ☐ Winner
- ☐ Win-Win Attitude
- ☐ Wisdom
- ☐ _____
- ☐ _____
- ☐ _____
- ☐ _____

Blank Leadership Wheel

Directions: In the blank sections of the wheel add your top 8 Leadership Values / Qualities from the previous assessment. For each section, circle the number that represents your current level of satisfaction in that area. The higher the number, the greater your level of satisfaction.

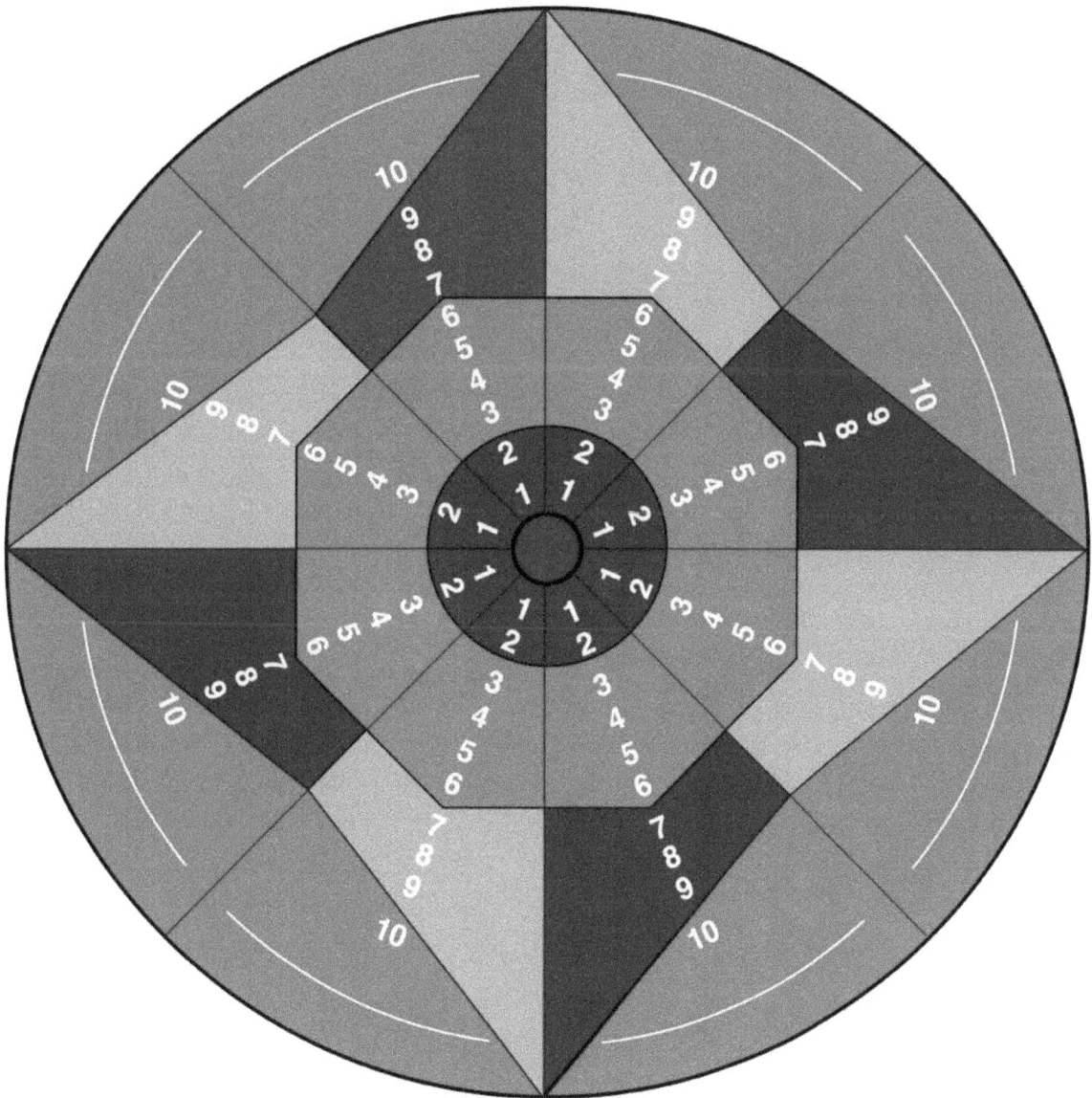

Leadership Quotes

If it is to be, it is up to me.
~ Anon

It is brave to be involved.
~ Gwendolyn Brooks

No pressure, no diamonds.
~ Mary Case

The best way out of a problem is through it.
~ Anon

I am a man of fixed and unbending principles, the first of which is to be flexible at all times.
~ Everett Dirksen

Everybody is talented, original, and has something important to say.
~ Brenda Ueland

Genius is an infinite capacity to take life by the scruff of the neck.
~ Katherine Hepburn

The manager accepts the status quo; the leader challenges it.
~ Walter Bennis

I was always looking outside myself for strength and confidence, but it comes from within. It was there all the time.
~Anna Freud

In times of change, learners inherit the Earth, while the learned find themselves beautifully equipped to deal with a world that no longer exists.
~ Eric Hoffer

You must unite your constituents around a common cause and connect with them as human beings.
~ James Kouzes & Barry Posner

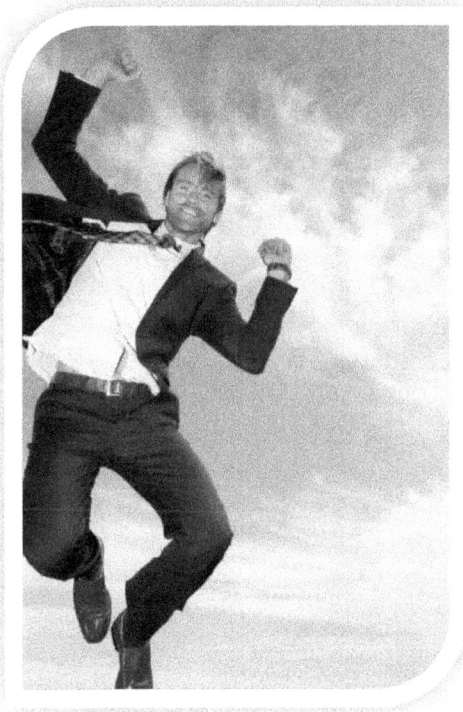

Every man is the architect of his own fortune.
~ Sallust

Try not to become a man of success, but rather a man of value.
~ Albert Einstein

I don't want to be a passenger in my
   own life.
~ Diane Ackerman

The only safe ship in a storm is leadership.
~ Faye Wattleton

What really matters is what you do with what you have.
~ Shirley Lord

The price of greatness is responsibility.
~ Winston Churchill

Leadership can be thought of as a capacity to define oneself to others in a way that clarifies and expands a vision of the future.
~ Edwin H. Friedman

I cannot give you the formula for success, but I can give you the formula for failure; which is: Try to please everybody.
~ Herbert B. Swope

A leader must have the courage to act against an expert's advice.
~ James Callaghan

If I have seen farther than others, it is because I was standing on the shoulder of giants.
~ Isaac Newton

Good leaders must first become good servants.
~ Robert Greenleaf

Time is neutral and does not change things. With courage and initiative, leaders change things.
~ Jesse Jackson

The manager asks how and when; the leader asks what and why.
~ Walter Bennis

If your actions inspire others to dream more, learn more, do more and become more, you are a leader.
~ John Quincy Adams

The world belongs to the energetic.
~ Ralph Waldo Emerson

A community is like a ship; everyone ought to be prepared to take the helm.
  ~ Henrik Ibsen

I suppose leadership at one time meant muscles; but today it means getting along with people.
  ~ Mohandas K. Gandhi

Most important, leaders can conceive and articulate goals that lift people out of their petty preoccupations and unite them in pursuit of objectives worthy of their best efforts.
  ~ John Gardner

Leadership involves finding a parade and getting in front of it.
  ~ John Naisbett

The very essence of leadership is that you have to have a vision.
  ~ Theodore Hesburgh

In leadership write large, mutually agreed upon purposes help people achieve consensus, assume responsibility, work for the common good, and build community.
  ~ Joseph Rost

The key to successful leadership today is influence, not authority.
  ~ Kenneth Blanchard

The final test of a leader is that he leaves behind him in other men the conviction and the will to carry on.
  ~ Walter Lipmann

Leaders are more powerful role models when they learn than when they teach.
~ Rosabeth Moss Kantor

Humans are ambitious and rational and proud. And we don't fall in line with people who don't respect us and who we don't believe have our best interests at heart. We are willing to follow leaders, but only to the extent that we believe they call on our best, not our worst.
~ Rachel Maddow

Divorced from ethics, leadership is reduced to management and politics to mere technique.
~ James Macgregor Burns

Trust your gut.
~ Barbara Walters

I start with the premise that the function of leadership is to produce more leaders, not more followers.
~ Ralph Nader

S.M.A.R.T. Goals Checklist

Specific

- ☐ What precisely is expected?
- ☐ Be as specific as possible.
- ☐ What will you have when the specific task is complete?
- ☐ What will the outcome be?

Measurable

- ☐ How would you know you have achieved success?
- ☐ How many tasks do you need to do?
- ☐ For how long?
- ☐ Make it a tangible process.

Achievable

- ☐ Is this achievable?
- ☐ What would be achievable?
- ☐ Do you have the skills or resources necessary to meet this goal?

Reasonable

- ☐ Is this a reasonable goal?
- ☐ What might be the obstacles?
- ☐ Considering everything else you have going on, can you achieve this goal?

Time-Oriented

- ☐ When will you be done?
- ☐ When will your tasks be scheduled?
- ☐ How long will it take to accomplish each task?
- ☐ When is the ideal time for this goal to be completed?

About the Work

We live in a time of great change. Faced with some of the most difficult challenges our world has ever known, we feel an urgency to find solutions to make our lives better. We want answers and we want them now!

In general, we focus on **getting the right answer not on asking the right questions.** Why is this? Perhaps it stems from an innate curiosity and a desire to make sense of the world. Perhaps it comes from a fear of the unknown or the need for a quick fix. It may also result from the need for blind acceptance of some *truth* where any form of questioning is strongly discouraged or denied. Perhaps we think we already have the answer, so why ask any questions at all? Whatever the case, there is no doubt human beings like answers.

When we focus on "getting the right answers," rather than "asking the right questions," we limit ourselves. We move into dualistic thinking: "I either have the right answer or I don't." We think in terms of yes or no, right or wrong, good or bad. **This black and white framework enables only surface inquiry**, at best, and quells deeper investigation and the ability to engage with others in meaningful ways. We lose the opportunity to generate new solutions to old problems.

Why are asking the right questions important? Because they generate beneficial lasting change. Empowering questions make possible diverse perspectives, which in turn lead to sustainable solutions to complicated challenges. They enable people to engage in dynamic transformational conversations out of which new ideas are born.

To generate the type of change our world needs, **we must raise penetrative questions to challenge current assumptions**; assumptions that keep us disempowered to affect change. The key in creating a positive, empowering future is asking positive, empowering questions now! So, what are you waiting for?

About the Authors

Kathy Jo Slusher, PCC, ELI-MP, Founder of Marketing Tao, LLC, has dedicated her life to help service-based socially conscious business owners make their business a success through sharing their passion. She believes that when your intention is on your passion and helping others, money is a natural bi-product. *It's not what you sell but what you stand for that makes you a success.* She is deeply committed to helping soloprofessionals and small business owners implement mindful marketing techniques and strategies to attract their ideal clients while making a difference in the world.

Kathy Jo is a Co-Founder of The REAL Results Coaching Exchange, partner in Coaching Skills for Leaders, a member of the International Coach Federation, and Vice-President of the United Nations Association of the US, Indianapolis Chapter.

Denny Balish, PCC, ELI-MP, Professional Certified Coach and Founder of ThreeFold Life Coaching, has dedicated her life's work to the development of Human Potential. She believes that each person has within themselves the desire and ability to be a positive force for change in the world and, by sharing one's unique gifts and talents with others, global change is possible. Denny is deeply committed to helping people and organizations get and stay powerfully on-purpose so they can be the change they wish to see in the world. Denny is a member of the International Coach Federation (ICF), Association for Global New Thought (AGNT), and founding board member of Spirit's Light Foundation, an alternative youth and family ministry with the Association of Unity Churches International.

Other Valuable Resources

For Coaches, Consultants, and Service-Based Small Businesses

Ultimate Questions Books

The real power in transformation is not in the answers, but in the questions we ask. If coaches, therapists or consultants are unsure of the questions to ask, client results are greatly impacted.

This series of books is specifically designed for coaches, consultants, therapists and others who are in a place where they need some fresh ideas to get themselves, a client, or anyone else unstuck. www.UltimateQuestionsBook.com

Marketing Made Practical

Marketing Made Practical is a Home Study Program designed for those who are overwhelmed with all the options and don't have a handle on how to make the marketing process into an effective, successful strategy.

Marketing Made Practical is specifically designed for service-based soloprofessionals or small business owners who are just getting started or have a limited experience and need an organized approach to marketing. www.MarketingMadePractical.com

Marketing Strategies University

Marketing Strategies University is an online training program that walks you through how to create a strong marketing and business development plan.

Marketing Strategies University cuts to the chase of marketing. We don't dive into the theory of marketing – but focus on practical steps to create and implement powerful marketing strategies.

This unique online training program is designed for service-based soloprofessionals or small business owners who have reached a certain level in their business where they are ready to create the systems and strategies for their marketing to take them to the next level of success. www.MarketingStrategiesUniversity.com

Marketing Strategies Success

Marketing Strategies Success is an online membership forum which brings together motivation and information into a community of like-minded business owners all working to create change through their business.

Through topic specific open Q & A calls & recordings, to an interactive forum where members share ideas, to a mentoring component of Success Stories, where successful entrepreneurs share their success secrets, this group will help those who have a message to share through their business but need marketing know-how & structure to accomplish their mission. www.MarketingStrategiesSuccess.com

For Leadership Development Support

Coaching Skills for Leaders

Employees don't leave companies, they leave managers.

According to the Gallup Poll, 71% of employees studied said they were either not engaged or actively disengaged at work. This employee disengagement results in $370 Billion lost annually. That's a huge amount.

In today's environment, talented individuals are arguably an organization's most valuable resource. Yet studies show, high potential employees have a higher turnover rate than any other employee population.

Leaders need to be flexible, adaptable, creative and resourceful to deal

with the reality of our economic times. Coaching Skills for Leaders will take you and your organization through The Coaching Clinic, a specialized training program where you acquire a new approach to old issues. This process offers a step-by-step process of a coaching conversation in how to conduct & lead those difficult conversations. You will learn how to address organizational challenges through a step-by-step structured approach to facilitate your own coaching conversation, and develop partners and accountability standards across the board. Thus you will be transforming managers into true Leaders. www.Coaching-Skills-for-Leaders.com

Lifestyle, Leadership, Legacy

What are you working for?

As a business owner or executive you've worked hard to get where you are at. But how has this helped the lifestyle you want to lead? If you're tired to living to work instead of working to live, this program is for you.

We will identify your desired lifestyle, look at how to improve your leadership ability so you can more effectively lead those around you as well as your own life and create a lasting legacy to leave behind.

On-Purpose Leadership Development

For on-purpose professionals who want to develop their leadership acumen while expanding their consciousness. This program formulates a plan of action to break through all obstacles limiting your success, while building powerful skills to help you lead with purpose, including: manage conflict and chaos with greater ease, use your intuition for effortless decision-making, communicate effectively and persuasively, maximize your ability to engage and influence people in positive ways, and feel empowered to affect change in yourself and others.

For Specialized Support for Non-Profits, Social Enterprises and Cultural Creatives

Life Purpose Coaching

Empowering individuals in their midlife years to create a life of deeper meaning and purpose by not only connecting with their authentic voice and innate wisdom, but also by helping them aligning their skills, talents and interests with their desire to give back in meaningful ways.

On-Purpose Career Transition

For individuals in all phases of career and job transition who seek to purposefully align their skills and abilities with their passion for a satisfying career; one that enables them to give back in meaningful ways. Make a living while making a difference! This program is customized to fit individual needs.

For More Information Contact:

Marketing Tao, LLC
Kathy Jo Slusher
Email   info@MarketingTao.com
Call   317.536.5544
Click   www.MarketingTao.com
Click   www.TheREALResultsCoachingExchange.com

Threefold Life
Denny Balish
Email   info@threefoldlife.com
Call   708.209.6977
Click   www.Threefoldlife.com